HAL LEONARD GUITAR METHOD

BLUES GUITAR SONGS

To access audio visit:
www.halleonard.com/mylibrary

Enter Code
5910-6161-3743-6884

ISBN 978-1-4234-1776-7

HAL•LEONARD® CORPORATION
7777 W. BLUEMOUND RD. P.O. BOX 13819 MILWAUKEE, WI 53213

Visit Hal Leonard Online at
www.halleonard.com

Boom Boom

Words and Music by John Lee Hooker

Tune up 1/2 step:
(low to high) E♯–A♯–D♯–G♯–B♯–E♯

Intro

Moderately ♩ = 158

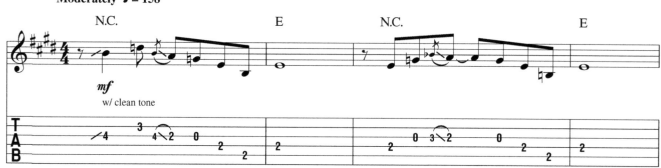

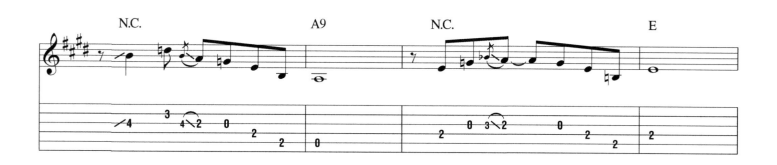

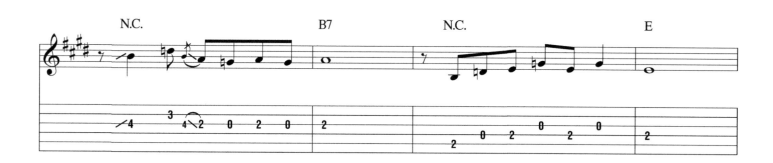

Verse

1. Boom, boom, boom, boom.　　I'm gon-na shoot you right　down, __

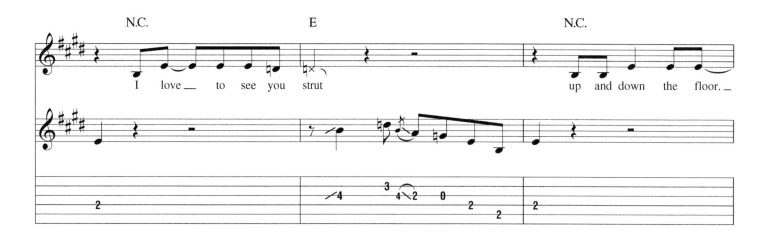

I love __ to see you strut up and down the floor. __

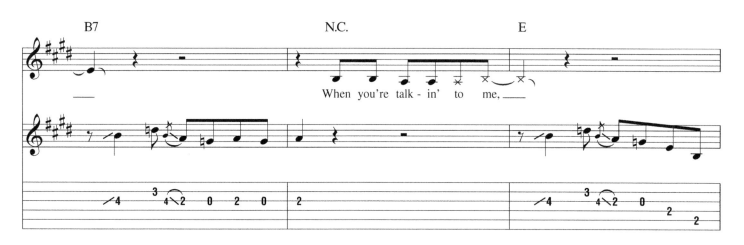

When you're talk - in' to me, __

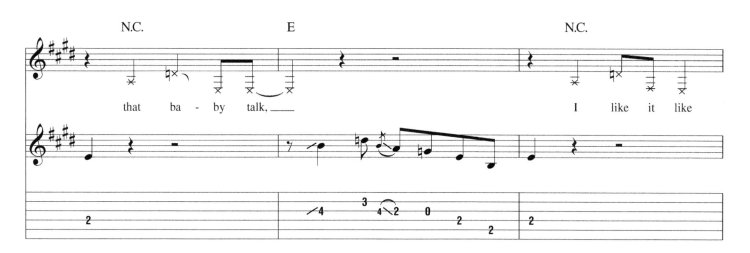

that ba - by talk, __ I like it like

To Coda ⊕

Guitar Solo

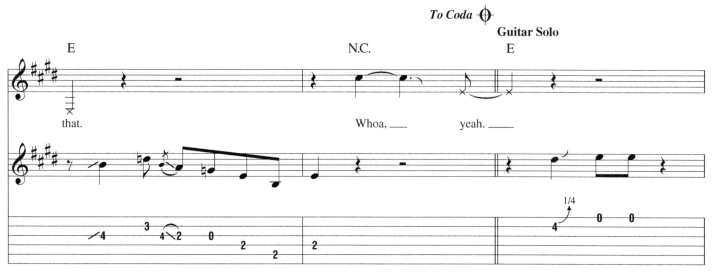

that. Whoa, __ yeah. __

Talk that talk!   Walk that walk!

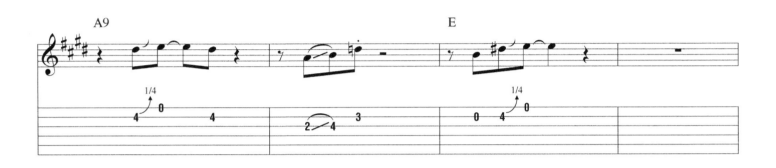

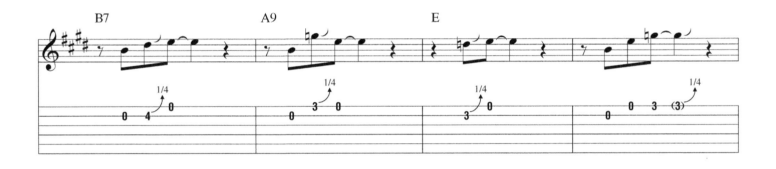

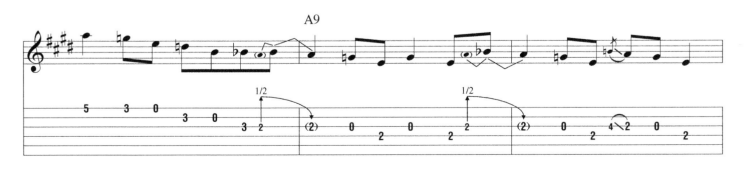

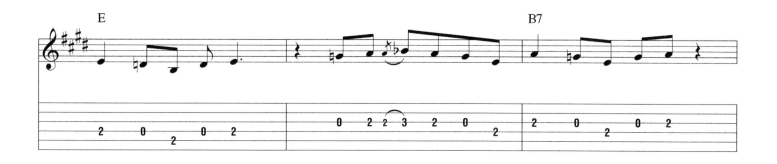

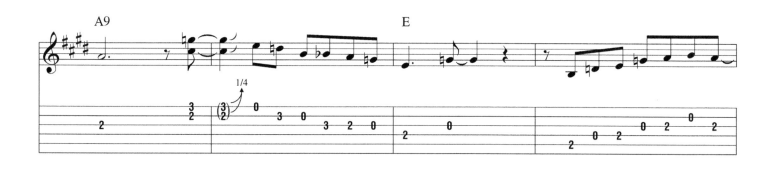

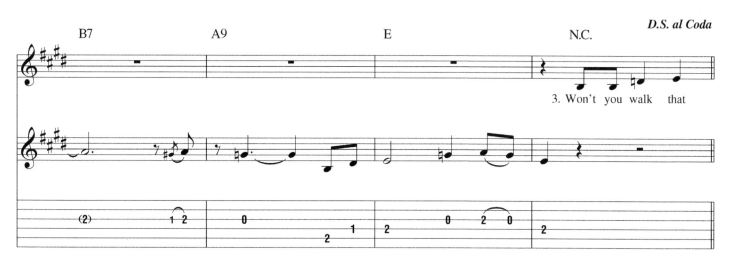

3. Won't you walk that

D.S. al Coda

Coda

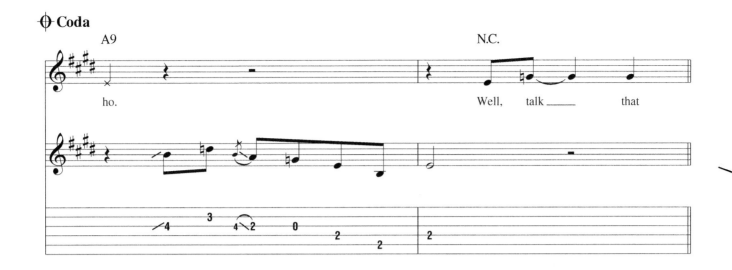

Outro

Begin fade

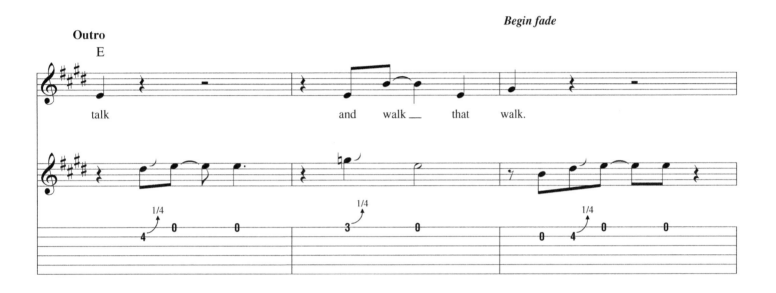

Fade out

Additional Lyrics

3. Won't you walk that walk and talk that talk?
   And whisper in my ear, tell me that you love me.
   I love that talk when you talk like that.
   You knocks me out, right off of my feet.
   Whoa, ho, ho, ho.

Born Under a Bad Sign

Words and Music by Booker T. Jones and William Bell

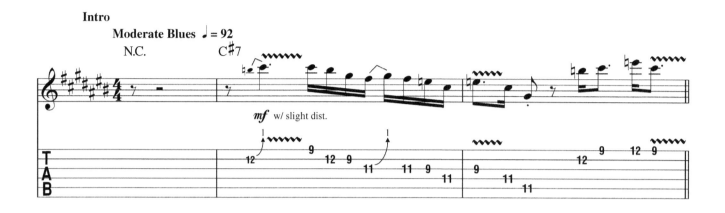

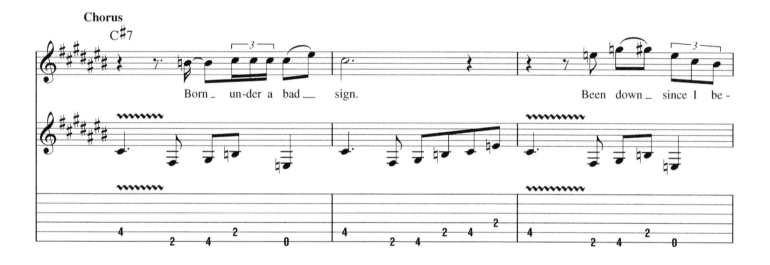

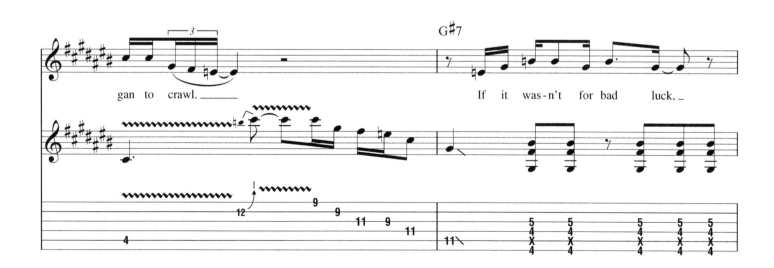

⊕ Coda

I tell you, I would-n't have no luck at all.

Outro

Yeah, I'm a bad luck boy! Been hav-in' bad luck all of

Repeat and fade

my days, yeah.

Additional Lyrics

3. You know wine and women
   Is all I crave.
   A big leg woman gonna carry me
   To my grave.

Hide Away

By Freddie King and Sonny Thompson

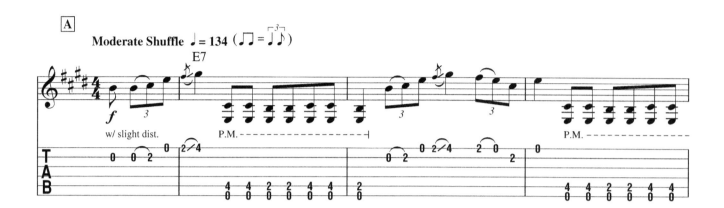

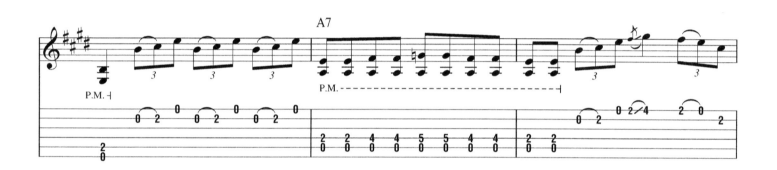

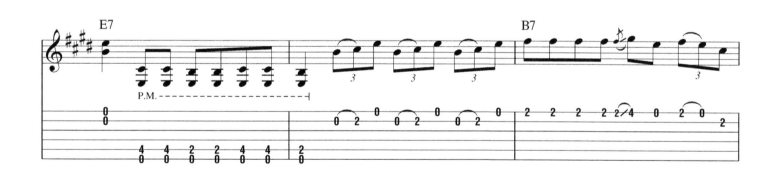

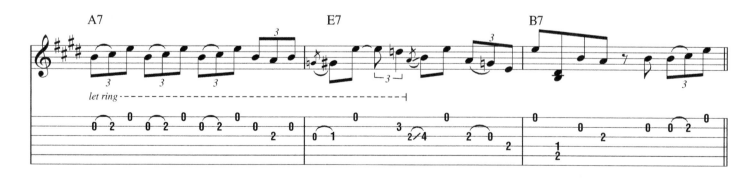

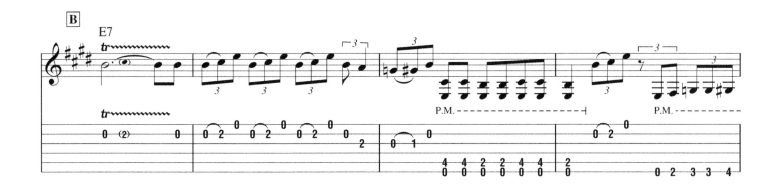

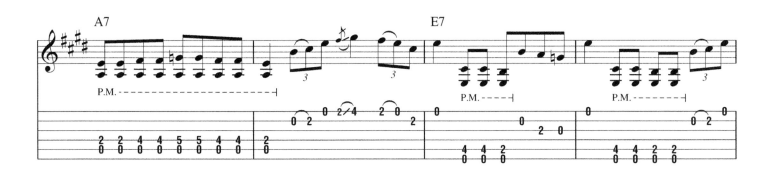

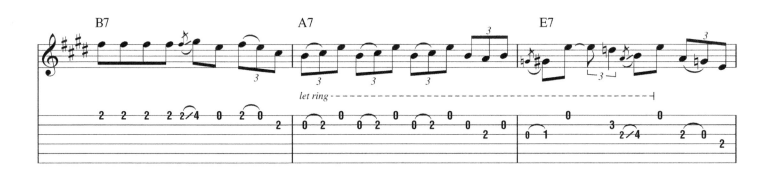

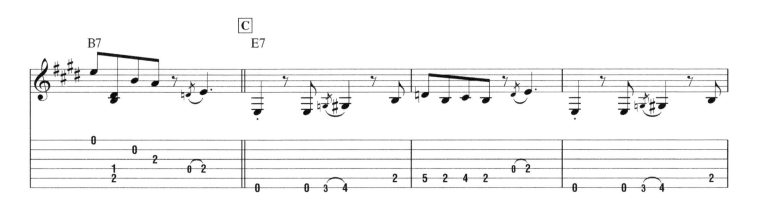

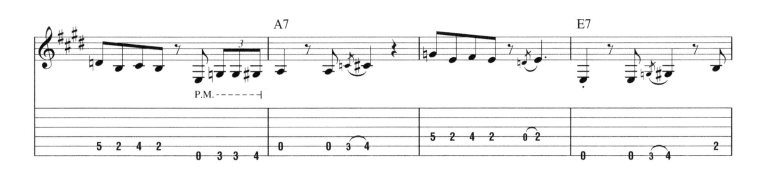

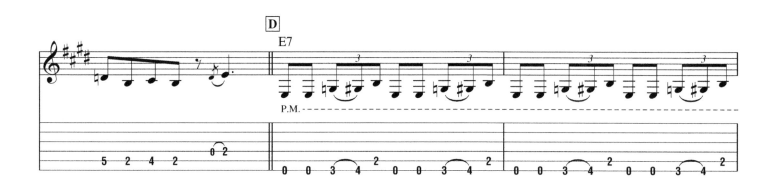

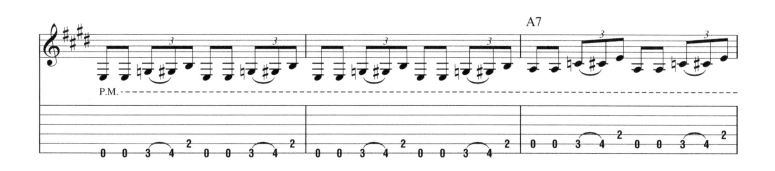

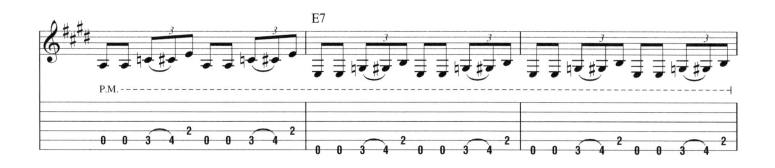

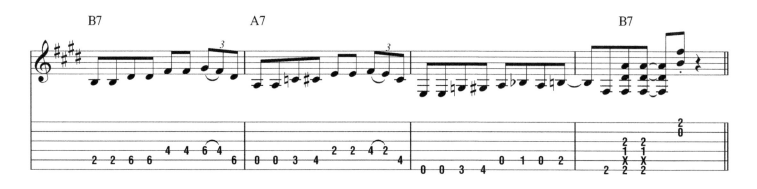

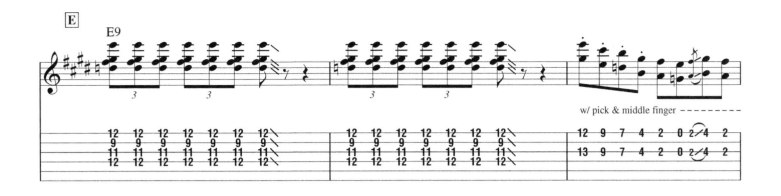

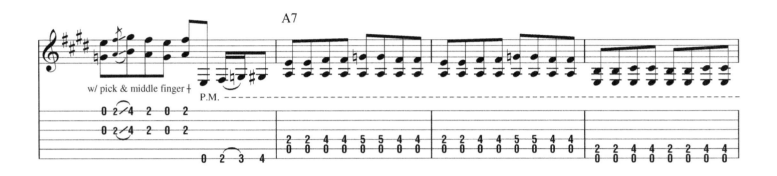

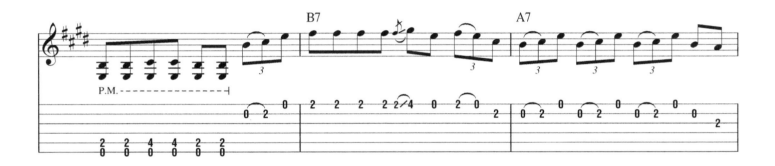

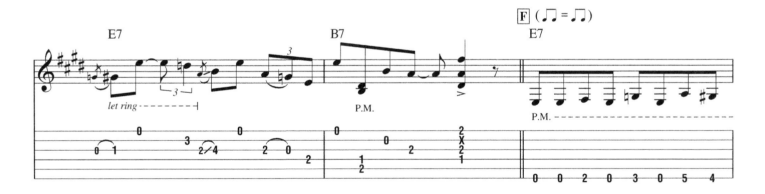

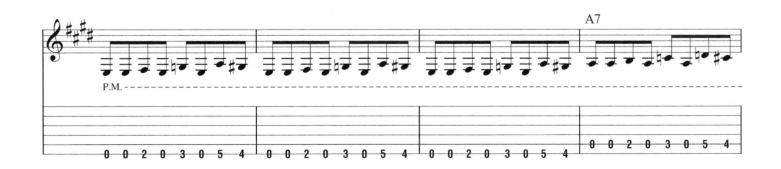

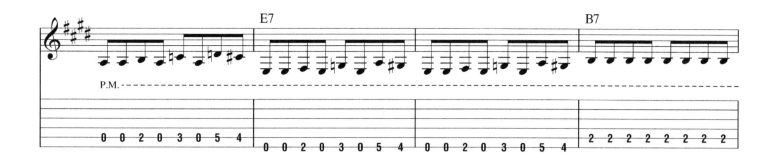

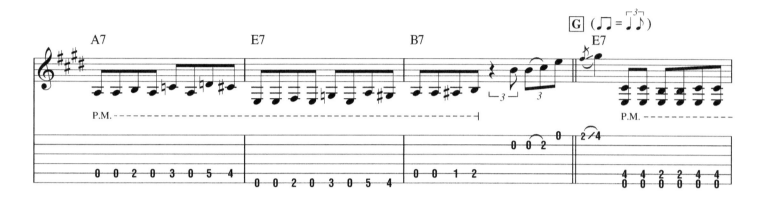

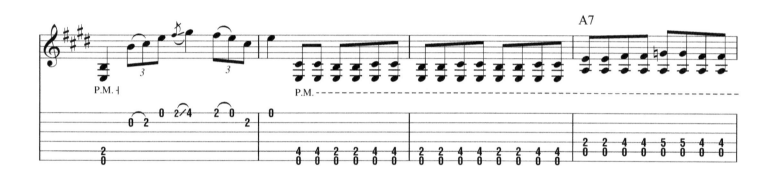

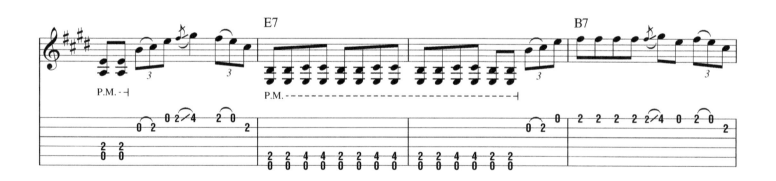

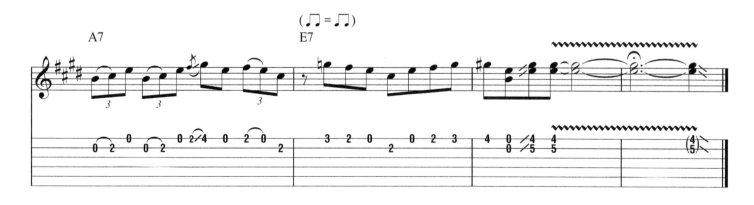

I'm Tore Down

Words and Music by Sonny Thompson

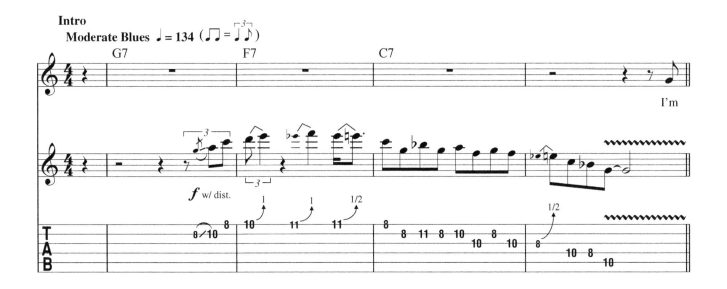

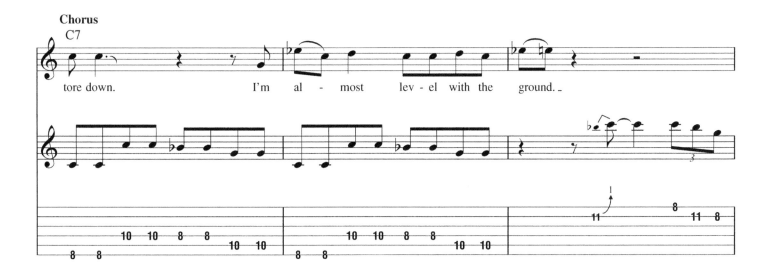

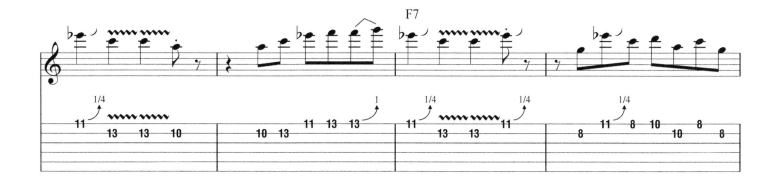

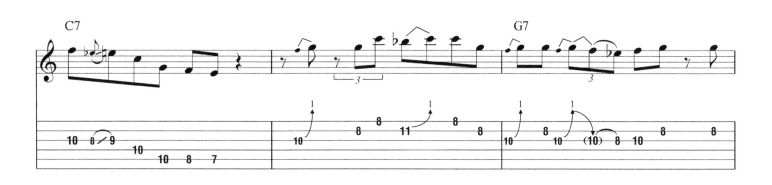

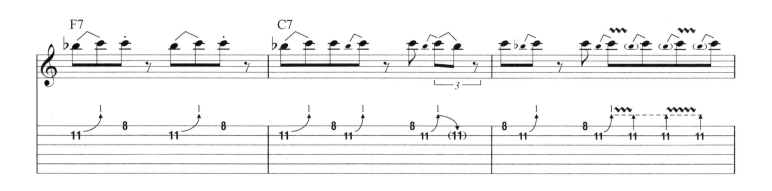

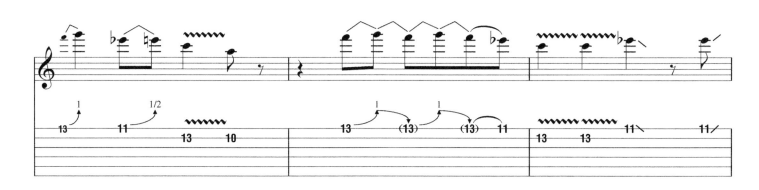

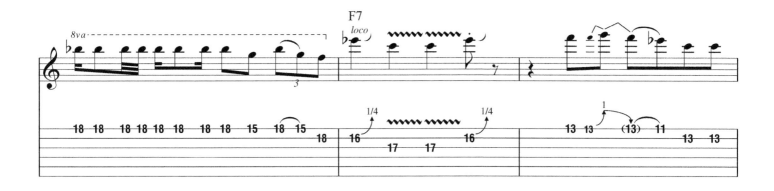

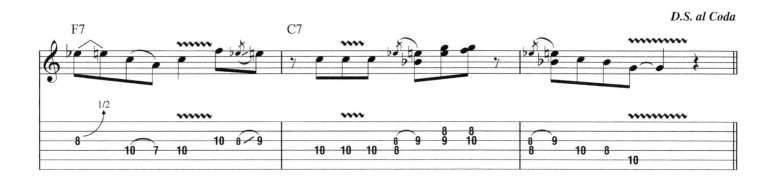

D.S. al Coda

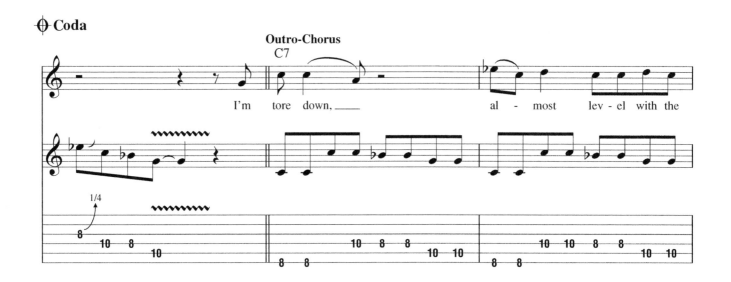

Outro-Chorus

I'm   tore   down, _____   al - most   lev - el   with   the

Additional Lyrics

3. Love you, baby, with all my might.
   Love like mine is outta sight.
   I'll lie for you if you want me to.
   I really don't believe that your love is true.

I'm Your Hoochie Coochie Man

Written by Willie Dixon

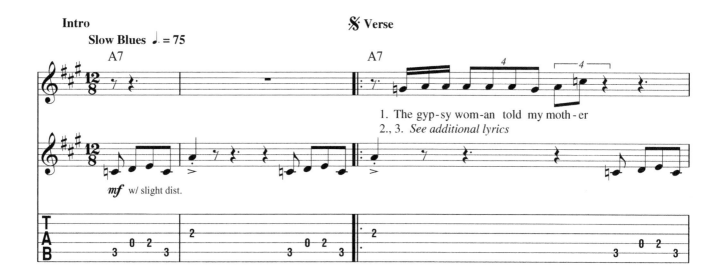

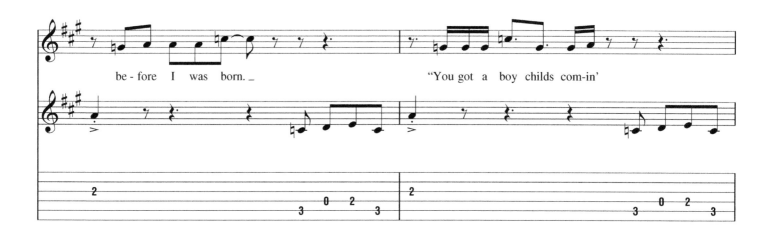

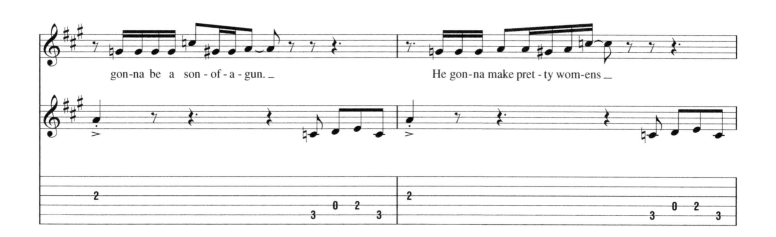

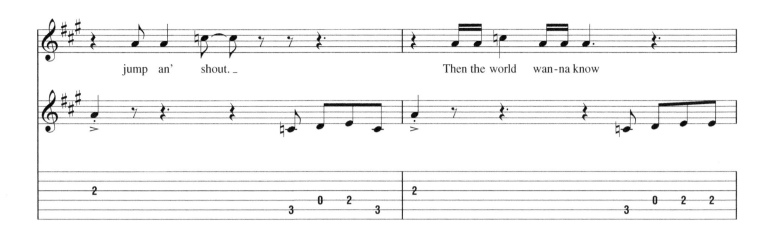

Chorus

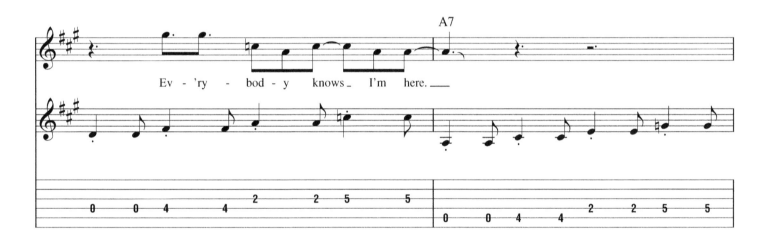

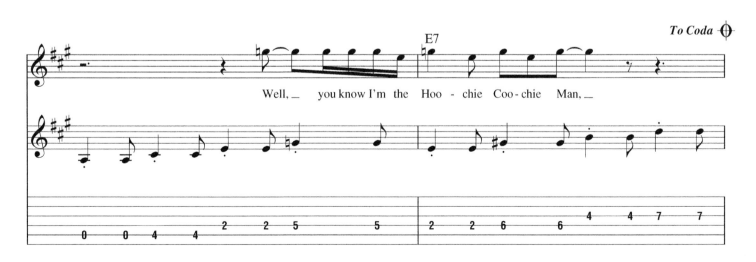

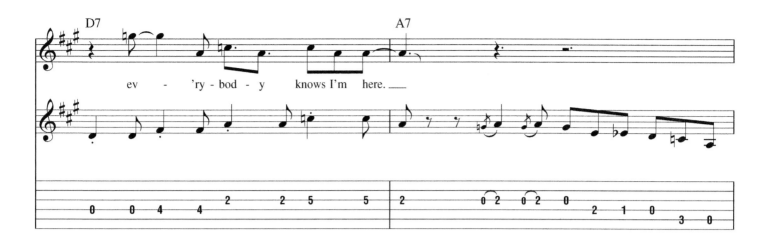

ev - 'ry - bod - y   knows I'm   here. ___

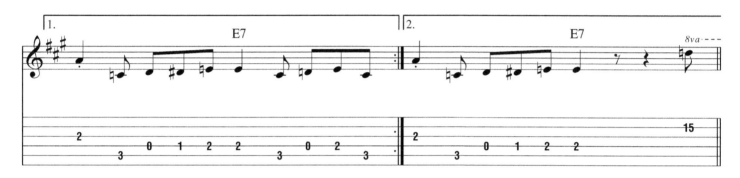

Guitar Solo

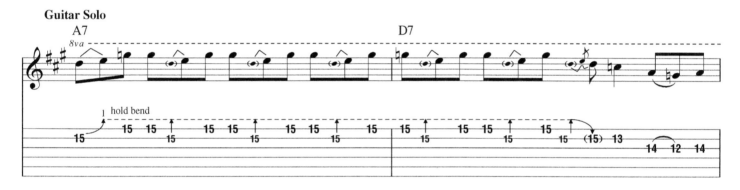

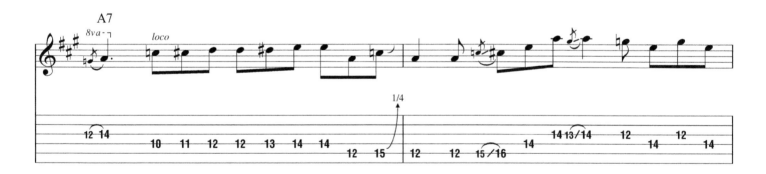

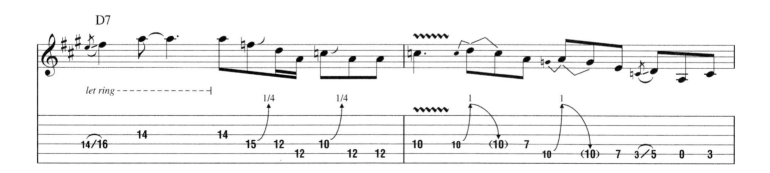

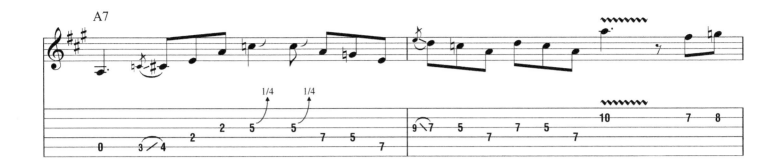

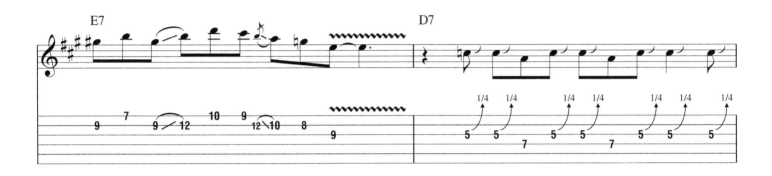

D.S. al Coda

Coda

the whole _round world knows I'm here.

Additional Lyrics

2. I got a black cat bone,
   I got a mojo too.
   I got the John the Conquerroot,
   I'm gonna mess with you.
   I'm gonna make you girls
   Lead me by my hand.
   Then the world'll know
   I'm the Hoochie Coochie man.

3. On the seventh hour,
   On the seventh day,
   On the seventh month,
   The seventh doctor say,
   "You were born for good luck,
   And that you'll see."
   I got seven hundred dollars,
   Don't you mess with me.

Killing Floor

Words and Music by Chester Burnett

Intro
Moderately ♩ = 120

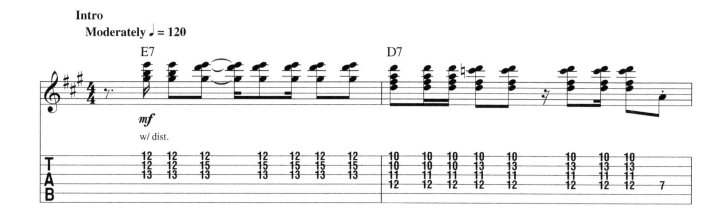

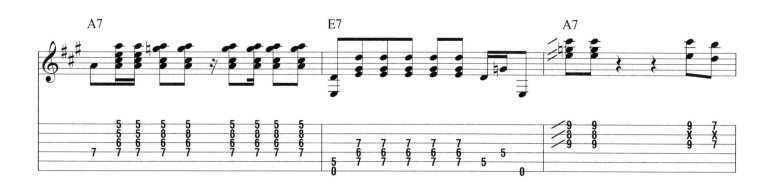

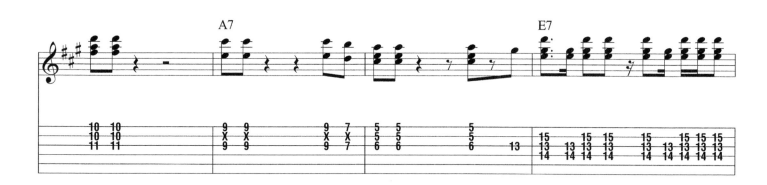

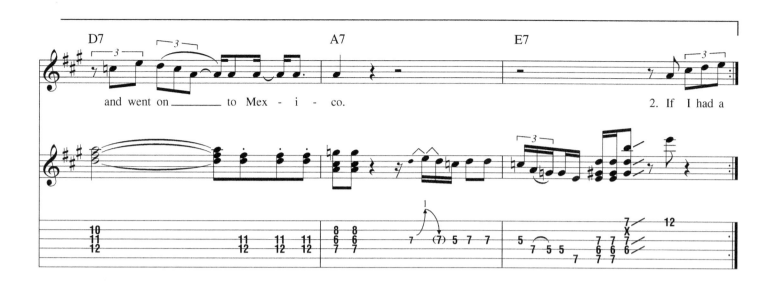

and went on _____ to Mex - i - co.

2. If I had a

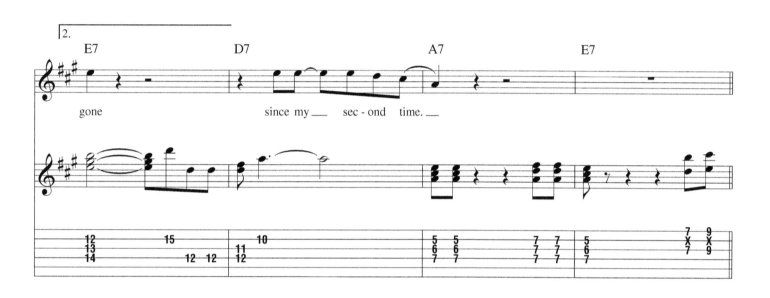

2.

gone

since my ___ sec - ond time. ___

Guitar Solo

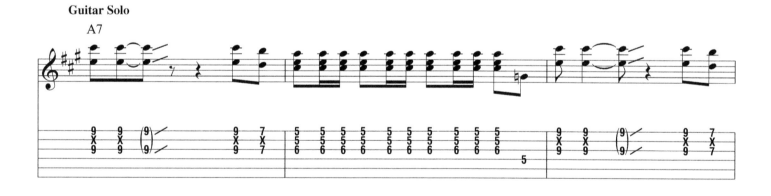

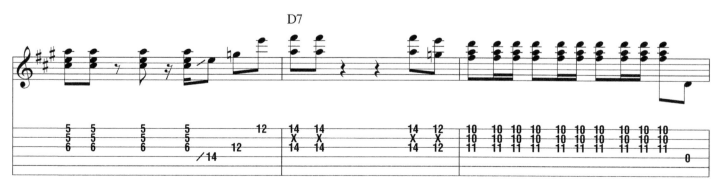

D.S. al Coda 1

3. I should have

⊕ Coda 1

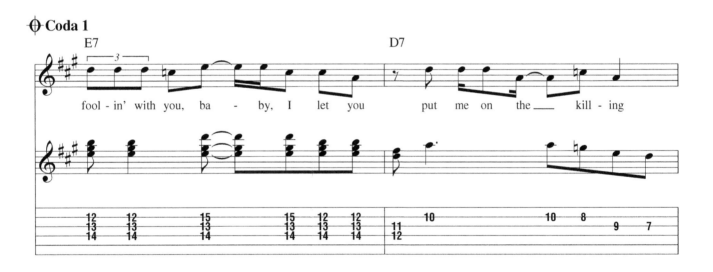

fool - in' with you, ba - by, I let you put me on the ___ kill - ing

D.S. al Coda 2

floor.   4. God knows ___

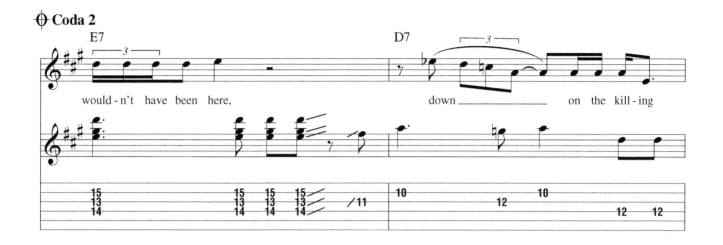

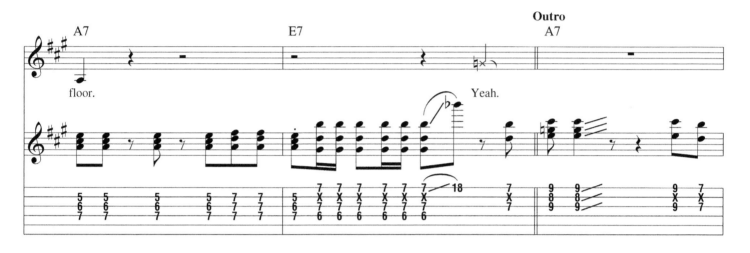

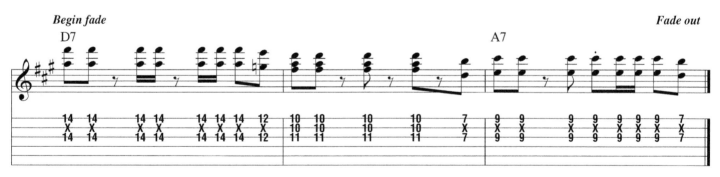

Additional Lyrics

2. If I had a followed my first mind,
   If I had a followed my first mind,
   I'd a been gone since my second time.

3. I should have went on when my friend come from Mexico at me.
   I should have went on when my friend come from Mexico at me.
   But now I'm foolin' with you, baby, I let you put me on the killing floor.

4. God knows I should have been gone.
   God knows I should have been gone.
   Then I wouldn't have been here, down on the killing floor.

The Thrill Is Gone

Words and Music by Roy Hawkins and Rick Darnell

Intro

Moderately slow Blues ♩ = 88

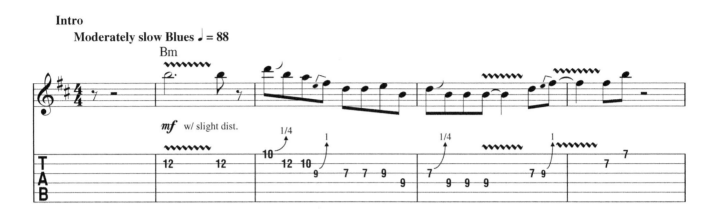

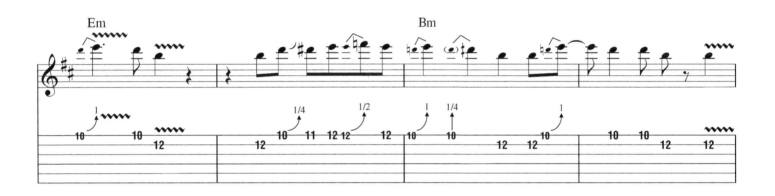

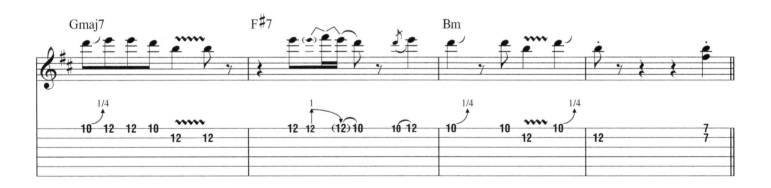

1. The thrill is gone, ___ the thrill is gone ___ a - way. ___
3. *See additional lyrics*

The thrill is gone,_____ ba - by,   the thrill is gone_____

_____ a - way._____   You know you done me wrong,_____ ba -

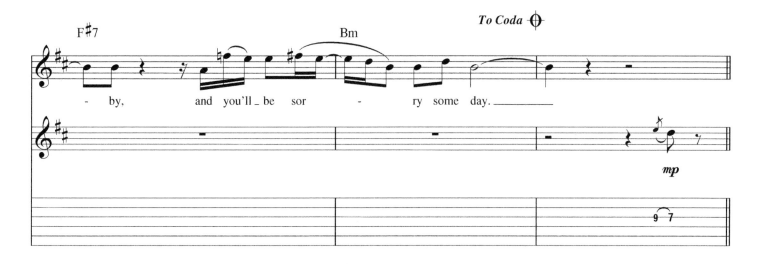

- by,   and you'll _ be sor - ry some day._____

To Coda ⊕

mp

Verse

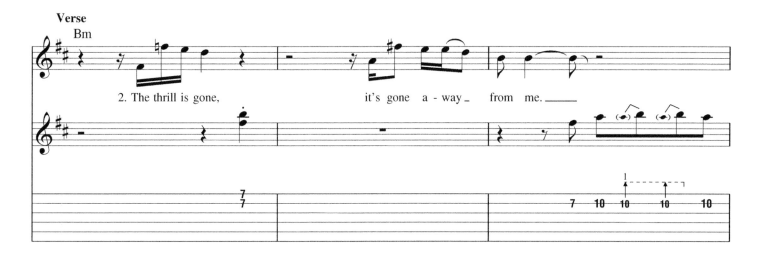

2. The thrill is gone,   it's gone a - way_ from me._____

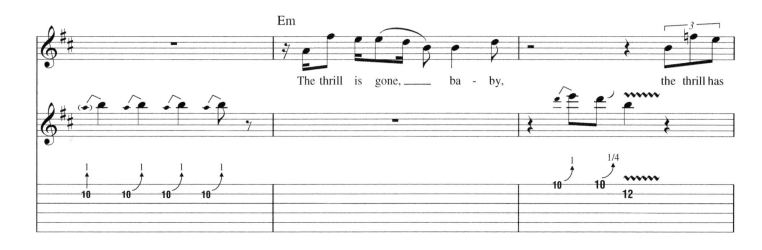

The thrill is gone,_____ ba - by,   the thrill has

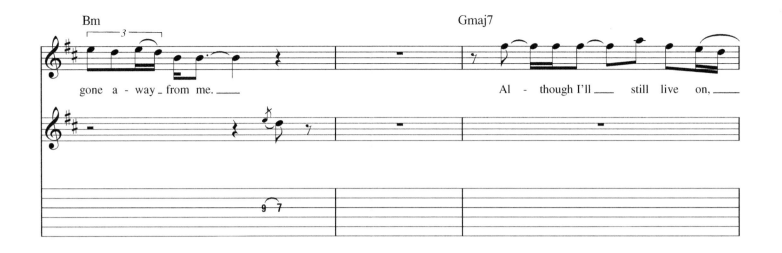

gone a - way from me. _____

Al - though I'll ___ still live on, ___

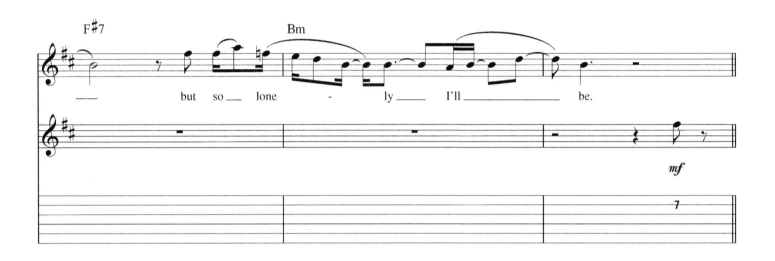

but so ___ lone - ly ___ I'll _____ be.

mf

Guitar Solo

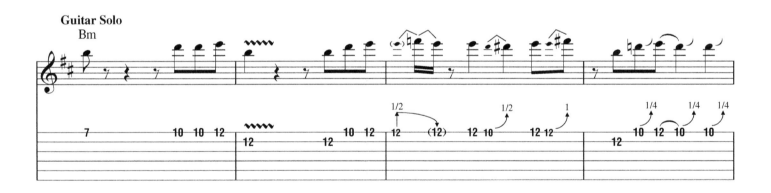

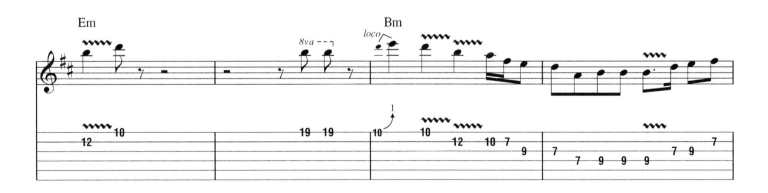

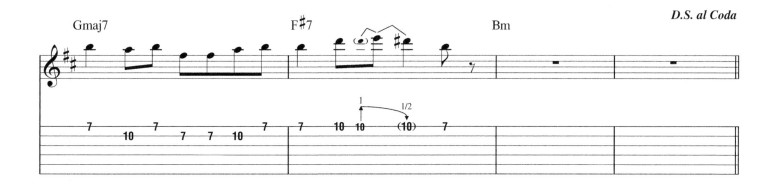

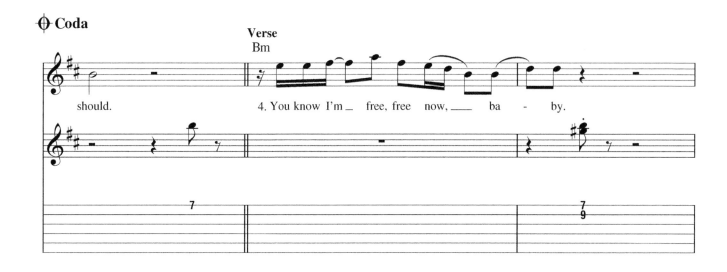

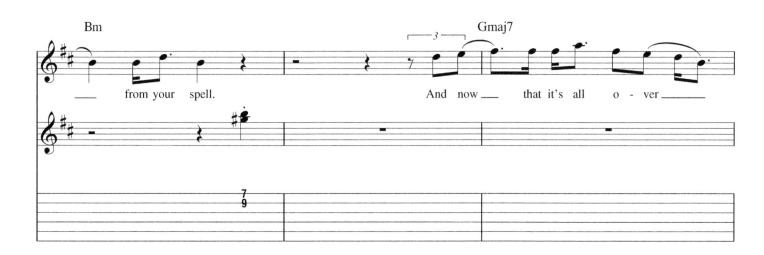

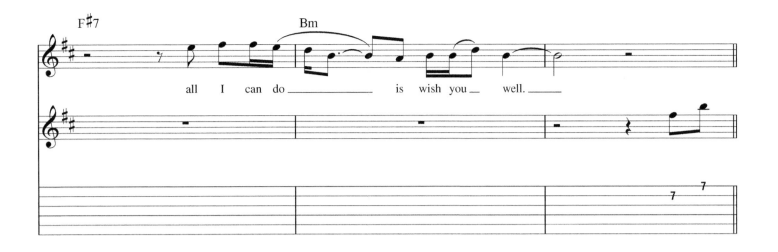

all   I   can do _____   is   wish you ____   well. _____

Outro-Guitar Solo

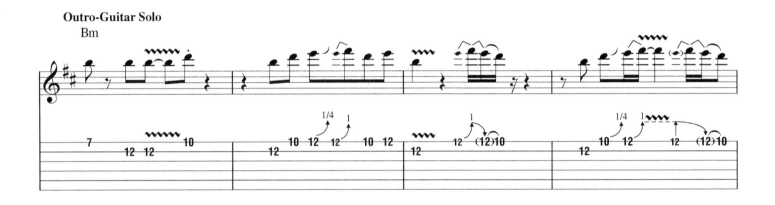

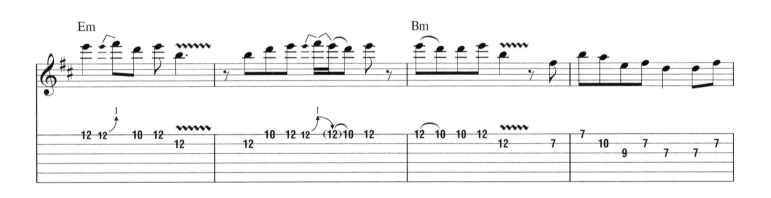

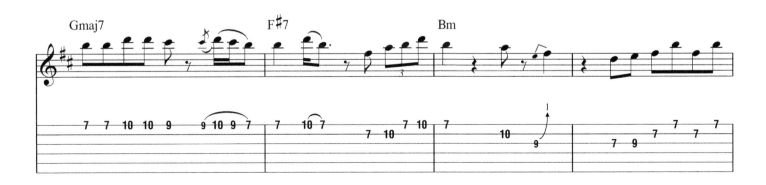

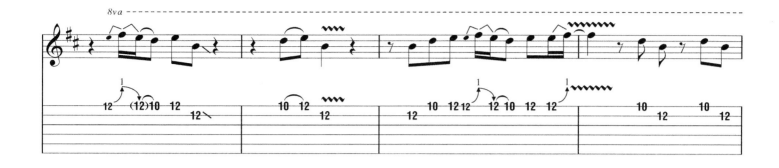

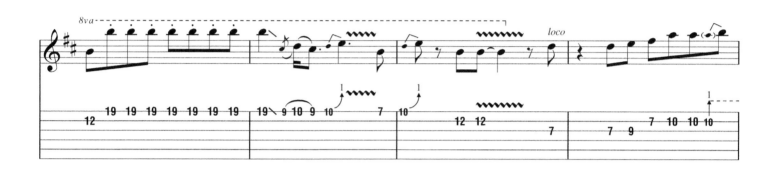

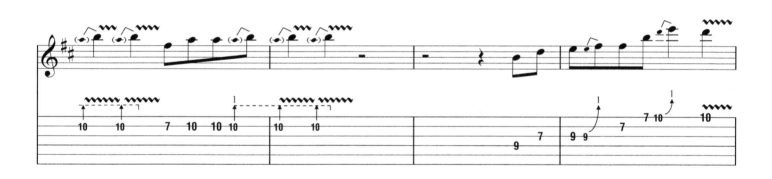

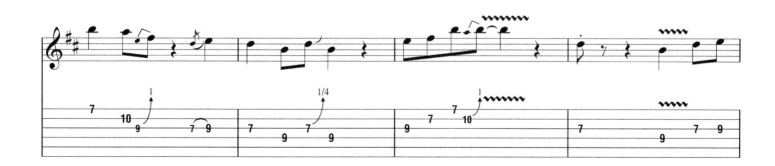

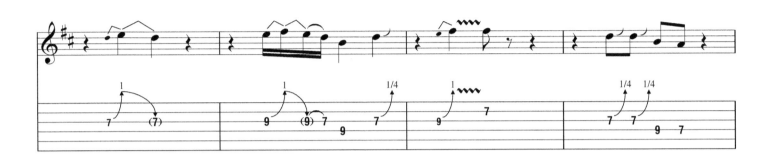

Begin fade

Fade out

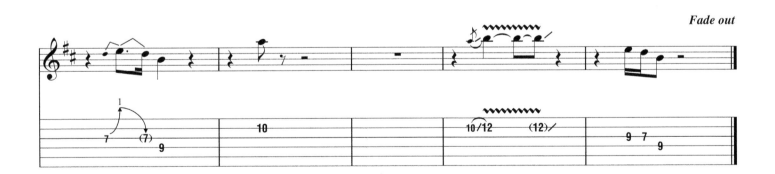

Additional Lyrics

3. The thrill is gone,
It's gone away for good.
Oh, the thrill is gone,
Baby, it's gone away for good.
Someday I know I'll be holdin' on, baby,
Just like I know a good man should.

Pride and Joy

Written by Stevie Ray Vaughan

Tune down 1/2 step:
(low to high) E♭-A♭-D♭-G♭-B♭-E♭

Intro

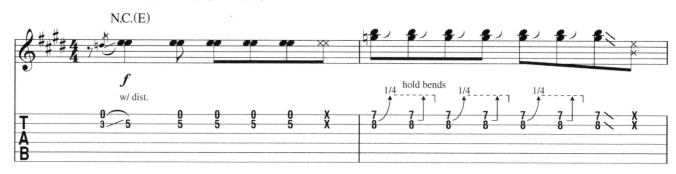

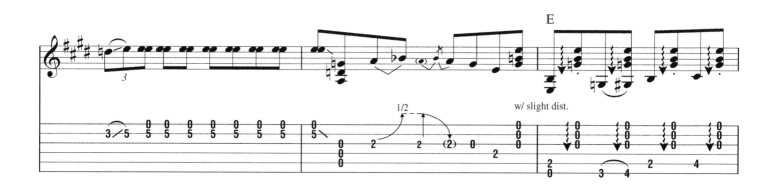

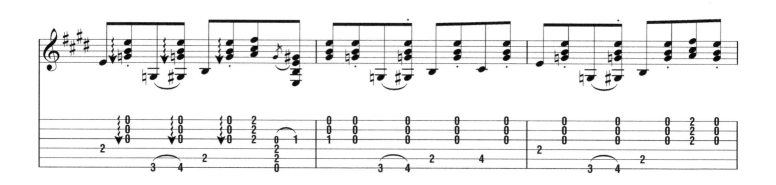

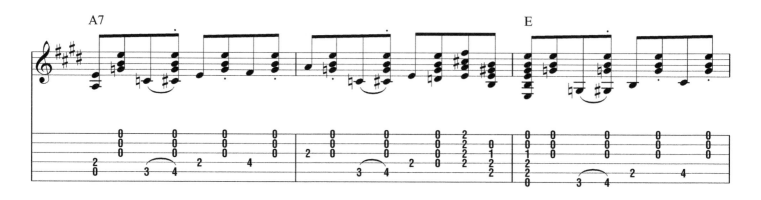

her _____ lit - tle lov - er boy. _____

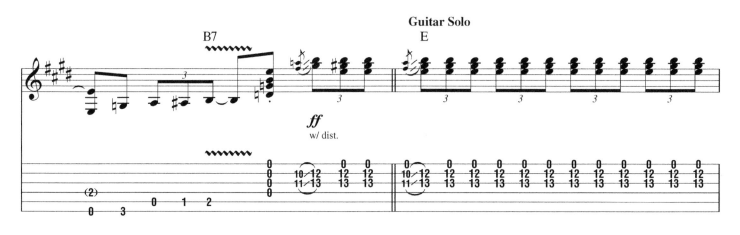

Guitar Solo

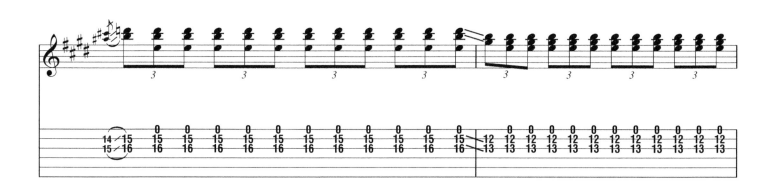

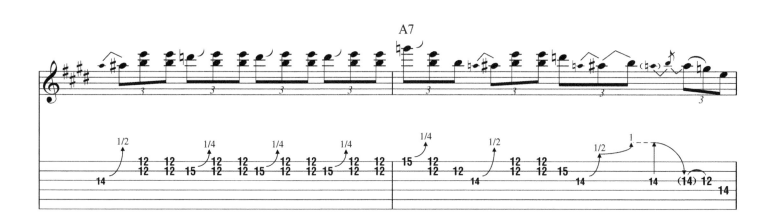

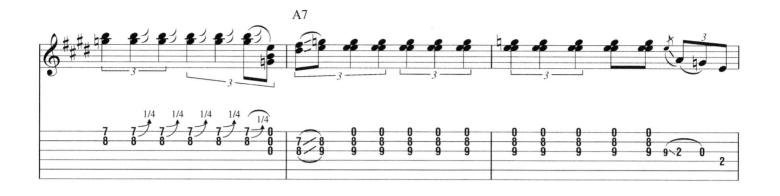

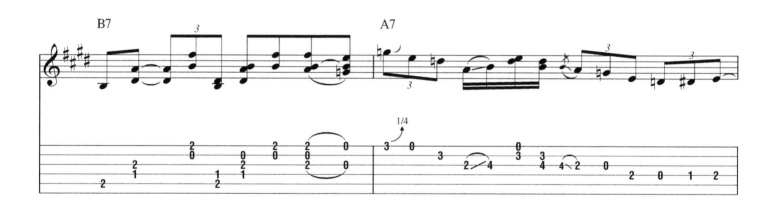

Guitar Solo

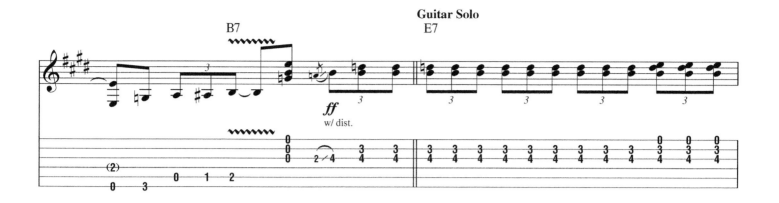

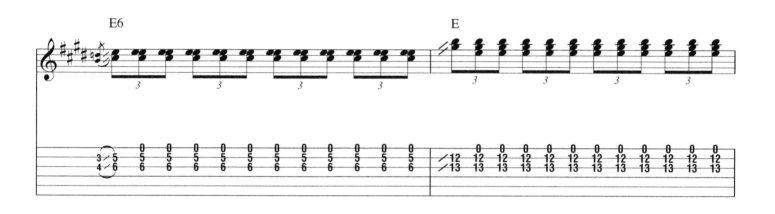

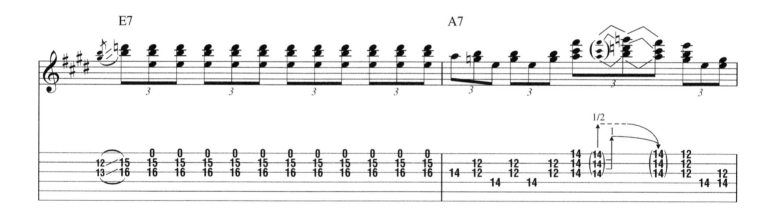

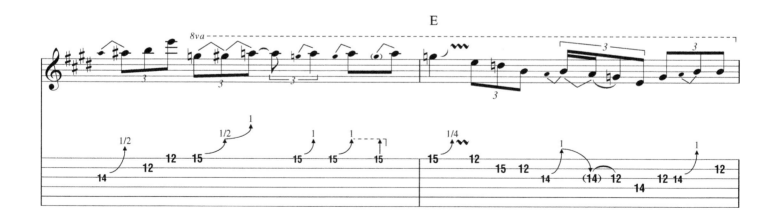

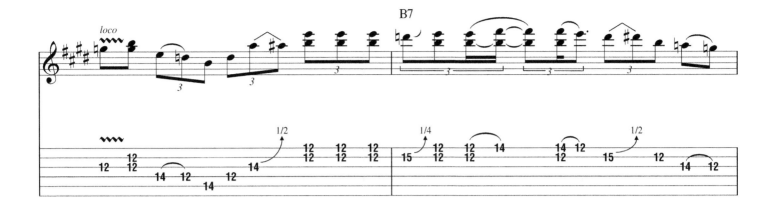

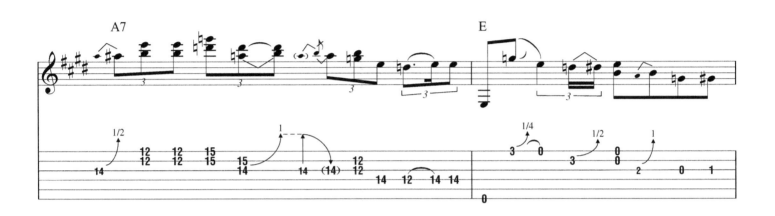

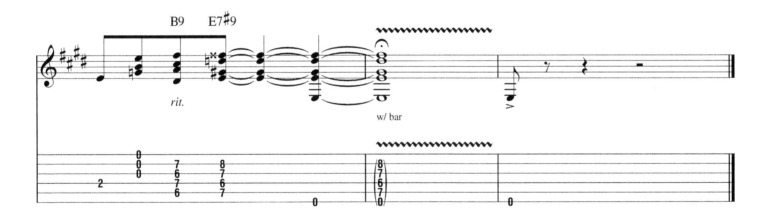

Additional Lyrics

2. Yeah, I love my baby, my heart and soul.
   Love like ours ah, won't never grow old.
   She('s) me sweet little thang,
   She('s) my pride and joy.
   She('s) my sweet little baby,
   I'm her little lover boy.

4. Well, I love my baby like the finest w, wine.
   Stick with her until the end of time.
   An' she's my sweet little thang,
   She('s) my pride and joy.
   She('s) my sweet little baby,
   I'm her little lover boy.

Sweet Home Chicago

Words and Music by Robert Johnson

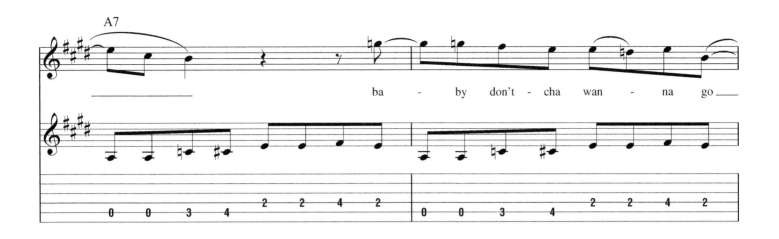

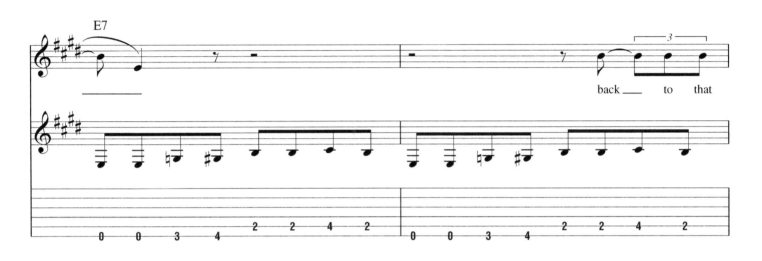

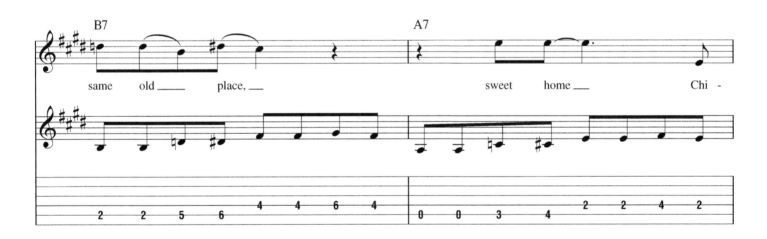

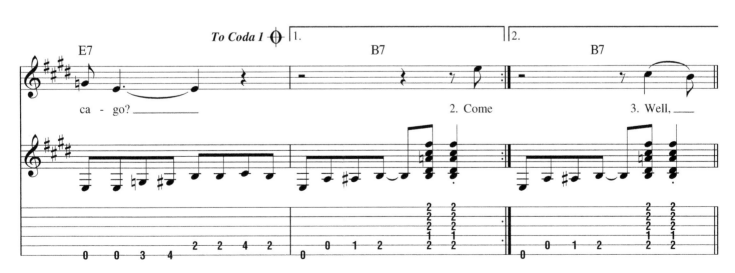

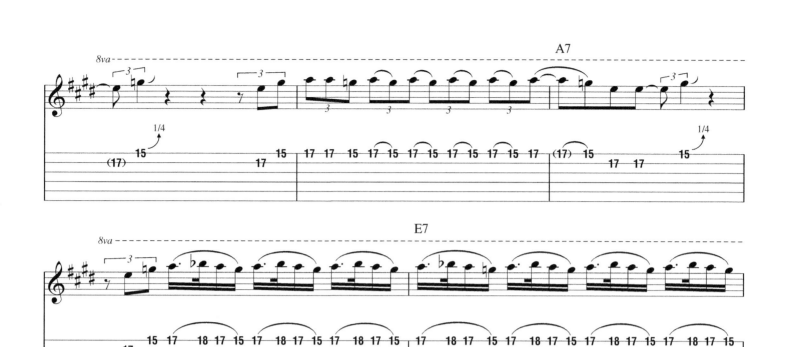

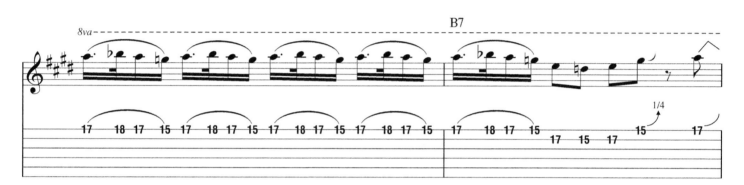

D.S.S. al Coda 2

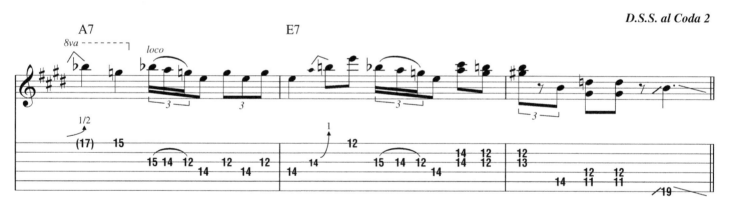

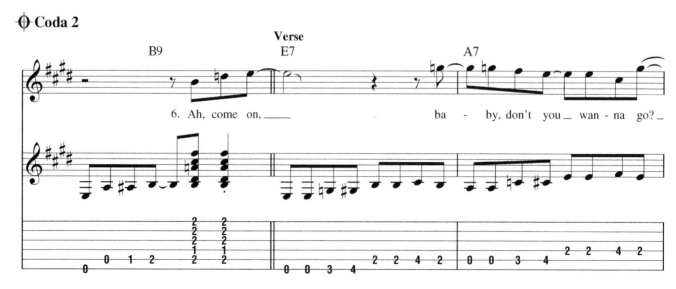

6. Ah, come on, _____ ba - by, don't you _ wan - na go? _

Texas Flood

Words and Music by Larry Davis and Joseph W. Scott

Tune down 1/2 step:
(low to high) E♭–A♭–D♭–G♭–B♭–E♭

Intro

Slowly ♩. = 68

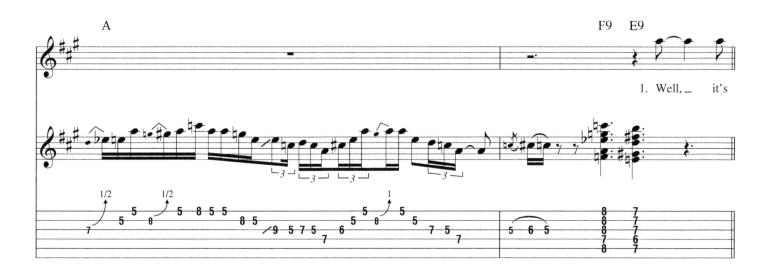

1. Well, __ it's

Verse

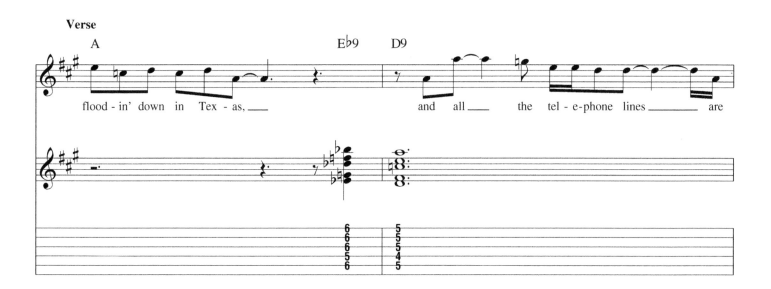

flood-in' down in Tex - as, __ and all __ the tel - e-phone lines __ are

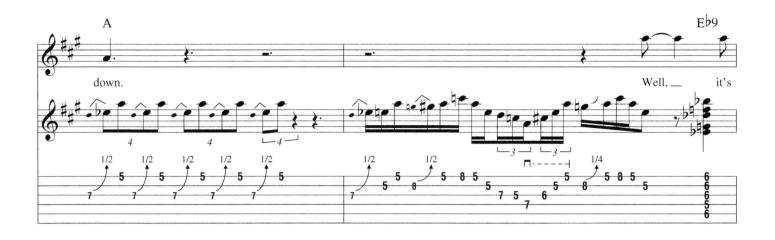

down. Well, it's

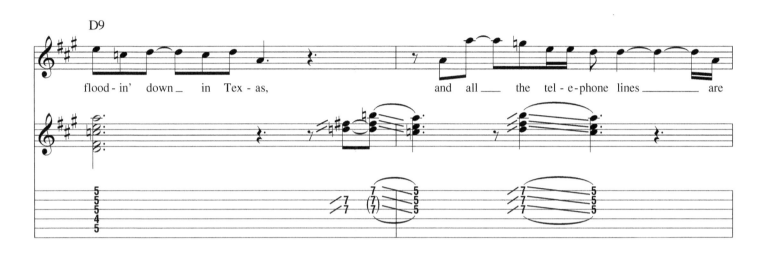

flood-in' down in Tex-as, and all the tel-e-phone lines are

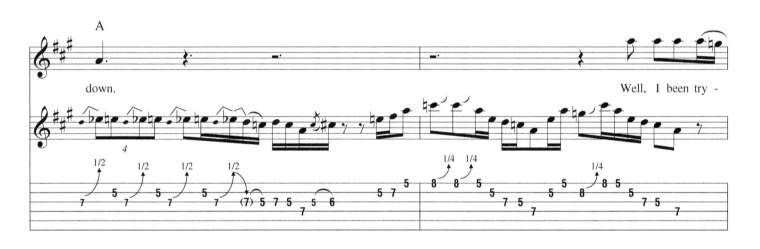

down. Well, I been try-

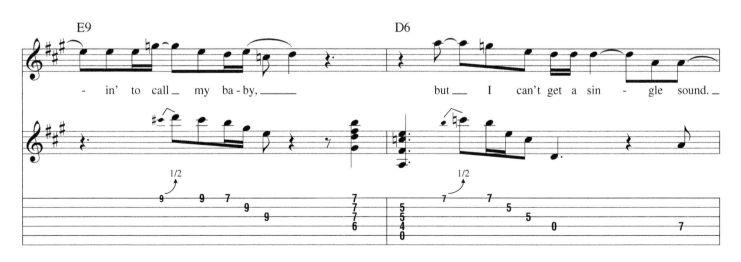

- in' to call my ba-by, but I can't get a sin-gle sound.

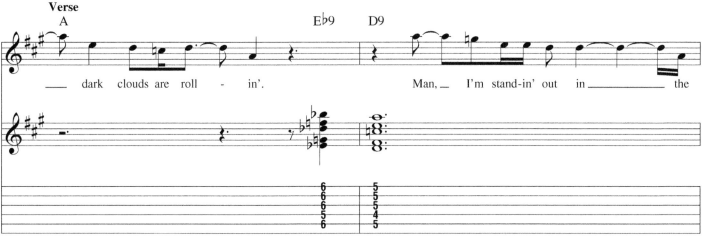

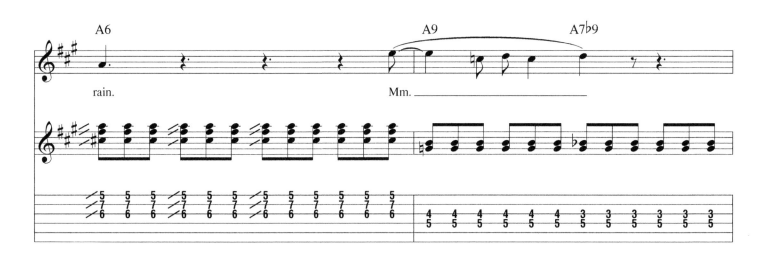

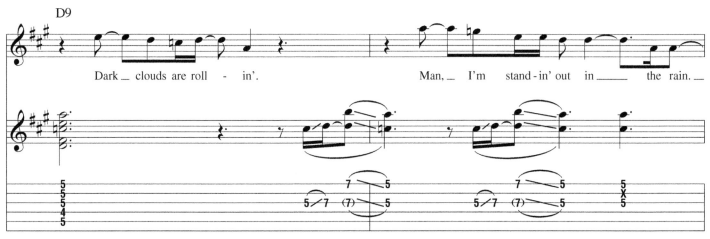

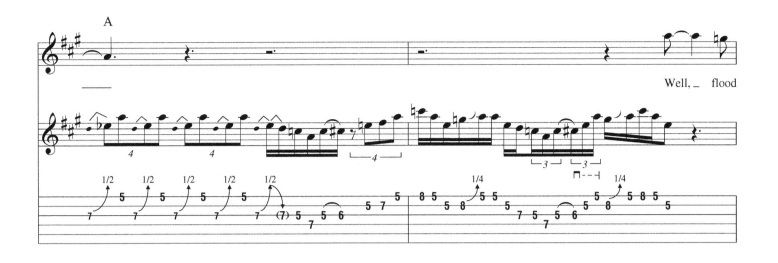

Well,__ flood

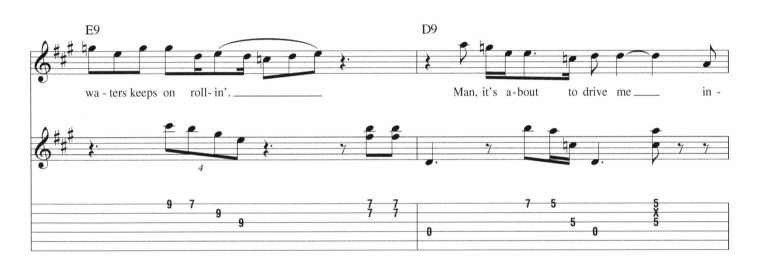

wa-ters keeps on roll-in'._____ Man, it's a-bout to drive me_____ in-

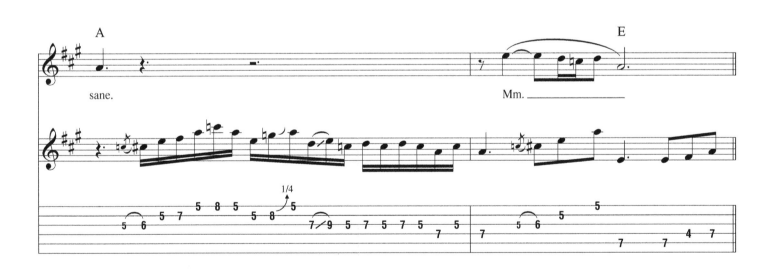

sane. Mm._____

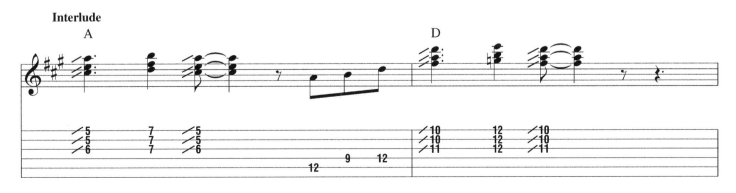

Interlude

Verse

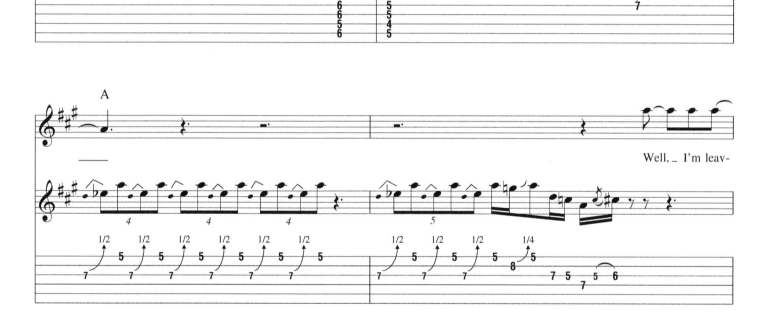

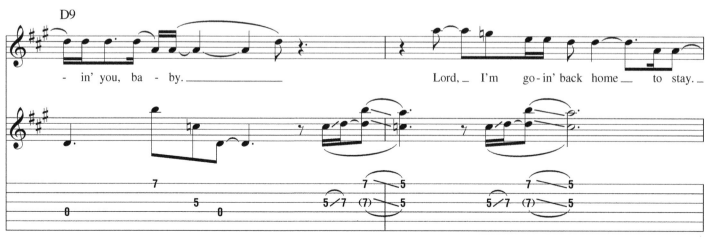

Guitar Notation Legend

THE MUSICAL STAFF shows pitches and rhythms and is divided by bar lines into measures. Pitches are named after the first seven letters of the alphabet.

TABLATURE graphically represents the guitar fingerboard. Each horizontal line represents a string, and each number represents a fret.

4th string, 2nd fret   1st & 2nd strings open, played together   open D chord

HALF-STEP BEND: Strike the note and bend up 1/2 step.

WHOLE-STEP BEND: Strike the note and bend up one step.

GRACE NOTE BEND: Strike the note and bend up as indicated. The first note does not take up any time.

SLIGHT (MICROTONE) BEND: Strike the note and bend up 1/4 step.

BEND AND RELEASE: Strike the note and bend up as indicated, then release back to the original note. Only the first note is struck.

PRE-BEND: Bend the note as indicated, then strike it.

VIBRATO: The string is vibrated by rapidly bending and releasing the note with the fretting hand.

PALM MUTING: The note is partially muted by the pick hand lightly touching the string(s) just before the bridge.

HAMMER-ON: Strike the first (lower) note with one finger, then sound the higher note (on the same string) with another finger by fretting it without picking.

PULL-OFF: Place both fingers on the notes to be sounded. Strike the first note and without picking, pull the finger off to sound the second (lower) note.

LEGATO SLIDE: Strike the first note and then slide the same fret-hand finger up or down to the second note. The second note is not struck.

SHIFT SLIDE: Same as legato slide, except the second note is struck.

PINCH HARMONIC: The note is fretted normally and a harmonic is produced by adding the edge of the thumb or the tip of the index finger of the pick hand to the normal pick attack.

TRILL: Very rapidly alternate between the notes indicated by continuously hammering on and pulling off.

TAPPING: Hammer ("tap") the fret indicated with the pick-hand index or middle finger and pull off to the note fretted by the fret hand.

NATURAL HARMONIC: Strike the note while the fret-hand lightly touches the string directly over the fret indicated.

TREMOLO PICKING: The note is picked as rapidly and continuously as possible.

VIBRATO BAR DIVE AND RETURN: The pitch of the note or chord is dropped a specified number of steps (in rhythm) then returned to the original pitch.

VIBRATO BAR SCOOP: Depress the bar just before striking the note, then quickly release the bar.

VIBRATO BAR DIP: Strike the note and then immediately drop a specified number of steps, then release back to the original pitch.

Additional Musical Definitions

(accent) • Accentuate note (play it louder)

Fill • Label used to identify a brief melodic figure which is to be inserted into the arrangement.

(staccato) • Play the note short

N.C. • No Chord

D.S. al Coda • Go back to the sign (𝄋), then play until the measure marked *"To Coda"*, then skip to the section labelled *"Coda."*

 • Repeat measures between signs.

D.C. al Fine • Go back to the beginning of the song and play until the measure marked *"Fine"* (end).

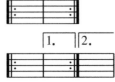 • When a repeated section has different endings, play the first ending only the first time and the second ending only the second time.

64